AF207001

discovermore
Your Government

The U.S. Constitution

Ezra E. Knopp

Britannica®
Educational Publishing

IN ASSOCIATION WITH

R THE ROSEN
PUBLISHING
GROUP

Published in 2024 by Britannica Educational Publishing (a trademark of Encyclopædia Britannica, Inc.) in association with The Rosen Publishing Group, Inc.
2544 Clinton Street, Buffalo, NY 14224

Distributed exclusively by Rosen Publishing.
To see additional Britannica Educational Publishing titles, go to rosenpublishing.com.

Editor: Caitie McAneney
Book Design: Rachel Rising

Photo Credits: Cover; (series background) Dai Yim/Shutterstock.com; Cover Mark R/Shutterstock.com; p. 4 JPL Designs/Shutterstock.com; pp. 5, 13, 25 Everett Collection/Shutterstock.com; p. 6 https://commons.wikimedia.org/wiki/File:Spirit_of_76%E2%A0%801912_Painting_by_Archibald_MacNeal_Willard.jpg; p. 7 https://commons.wikimedia.org/wiki/File:John_Dickinson_-_engraved_by_J.B._Forrest_from_a_portrait_by_C.W._Peale_painted_in_1770._LCCN2001699826.jpg; p. 8 https://commons.wikimedia.org/wiki/File:Scene_at_the_Signing_of_the_Constitution_of_the_United_States.jpg; p. 9 Kamira/Shutterstock.com; p. 11 https://commons.wikimedia.org/wiki/File:James_Madison,_fourth_President_of_the_United_States_LCCN2017660714.jpg; p. 11 f11photo/Shutterstock.com; p. 12 https://commons.wikimedia.org/wiki/File:On_Board_a_Slave-Ship,_engraving_by_Swain_c._1835.jpg; p. 15 Traci L. Clever/Shutterstock.com; p. 15 Salma Bashir Motiwala/Shutterstock.com; p. 16 travelview/Shutterstock.com; p. 17 larry1235/Shutterstock.com; p. 19 https://commons.wikimedia.org/wiki/File:President_Joe_Biden_and_Vice_President_Kamala_Harris_with_disability_advocate_and_artist_Tyree_Brown.jpg; p. 19 Postmodern Studio/Shutterstock.com; p. 20 https://commons.wikimedia.org/wiki/File:Plaque_of_Marbury_v._Madison_at_SCOTUS_Building.JPG; p. 21 https://commons.wikimedia.org/wiki/File:Supreme_Court_of_the_United_States_-_Roberts_Court_2022.jpg; p. 22 bodrumsurf/Shutterstock.com; p. 23 mireiasantiagophoto/Shutterstock.com; p. 24 Antwon McMullen/Shutterstock.com; p. 26 Rawpixel.com/Shutterstock.com; p. 27 ArtMediaWorx/Shutterstock.com; p. 28 YamabikaY/Shutterstock.com; p. 29 VGstockstudio/Shutterstock.com.

Cataloguing-in-Publication Data

Names: Knopp, Ezra E.
Title: The U.S. Constitution / Ezra E. Knopp.
Description: New York : Britannica Educational Publishing, in Association with Rosen Educational Services. 2024. | Series: Discover more: your government | Includes glossary and index.
Identifiers: ISBN 9781642829051 (library bound) | ISBN 9781642829044 (pbk) | ISBN 9781642829068 (ebook)
Subjects: LCSH: Constitutional law--United States--Juvenile literature.
Classification: LCC KF4550.Z9 K66 2024 | DDC 342.73–dc23

Manufactured in the United States of America

Some of the images in this book illustrate individuals who are models. The depictions do not imply actual situations or events.

CPSIA Compliance Information: Batch #CSBRIT24. For further information contact Rosen Publishing at 1-800-237-9932.

Find us on 

Contents

A Powerful Document

Many documents are important in understanding the history and government of the United States. None, however, are as powerful as the U.S. Constitution. This document describes the basic laws of the United States. Laws are the rules made by a government. All local, state, and national laws must agree with the U.S. Constitution.

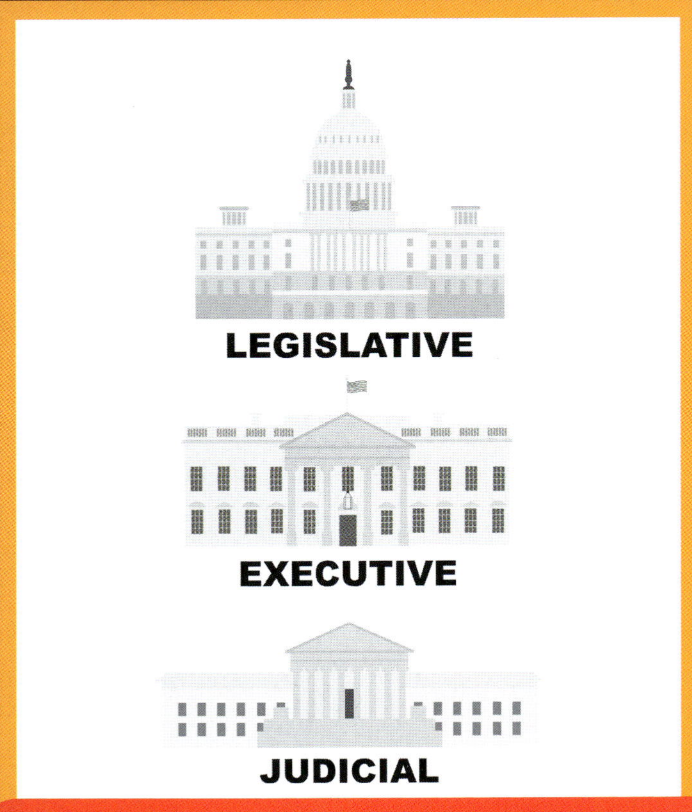

The three branches of government have separate powers, granted by the Constitution.

The Constitution also set up the government as we know it today. It created a federal system for the country. This means that the national government has certain powers and the states have other powers. It split the powers of the federal government into three branches: legislative to make laws, executive to pass laws, and judicial to decide if laws are fair and followed. The U.S. Constitution is still used every day to keep the government running.

Consider This

The Constitution was inspired by documents that came before it. One important one was England's Magna Carta, signed in 1215. It guaranteed basic rights to English people.

The Articles of Confederation

Today's Constitution wasn't the first constitution of the United States. Before that, the Articles of Confederation was used. It was written after the 13 North American colonies declared their independence from Great Britain. It went into effect in 1781.

After Americans won independence from the British government, they were nervous about having a powerful central government.

The Articles of Confederation didn't work well. This document gave the United States a weak national government and strong state governments. Congress had no way to enforce its power and could not make states follow the laws. After only a few years, the nation's leaders started talking about ways to improve the Articles of Confederation. It was time for the Constitutional Convention.

Consider This

Congress couldn't raise money through collecting taxes under the Articles of Confederation. It could only ask the states for money. Why might this be ineffective?

Creating the Constitution

Delegates from every state except Rhode Island came to the Constitutional Convention. They met in Philadelphia, Pennsylvania, from May 25 to September 17, 1787. The convention was called so that these delegates could talk about improving the way that the U.S. government worked.

George Washington was chosen to lead the Constitutional Convention.

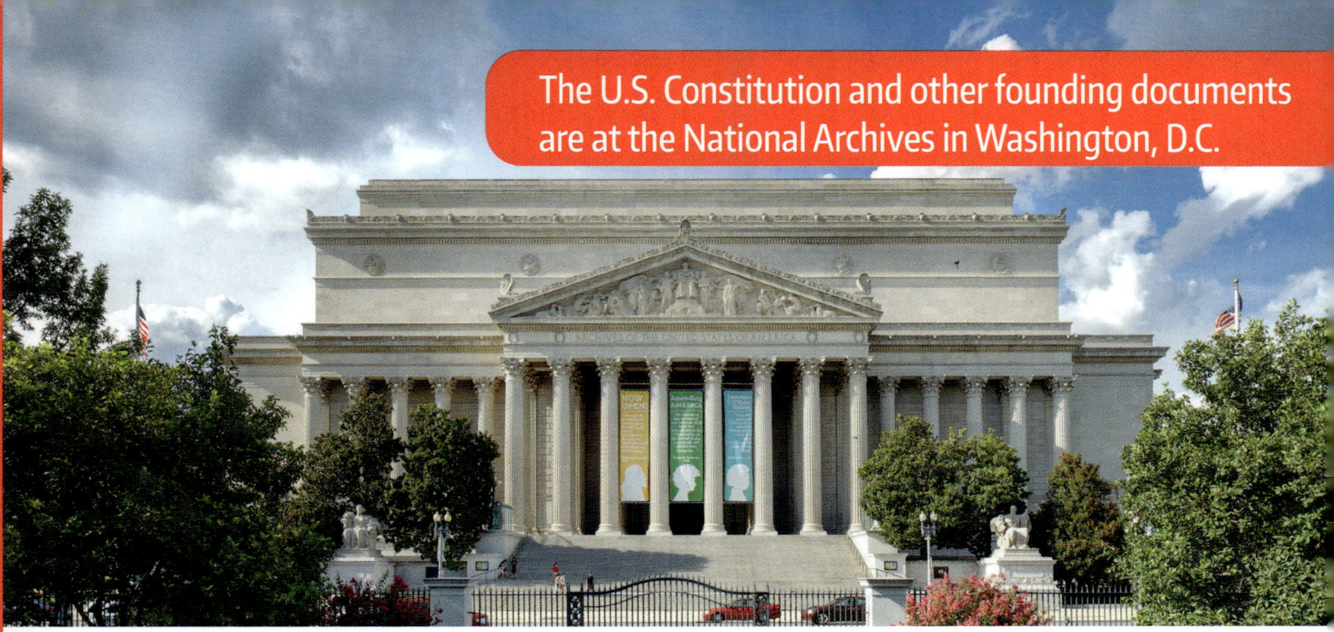

The U.S. Constitution and other founding documents are at the National Archives in Washington, D.C.

Many **Founding Fathers** were there as representatives of their states. These well-known representatives included Benjamin Franklin, Alexander Hamilton, and James Madison. They first met to revise, or fix, the Articles of Confederation, but soon decided to discard it completely. Their goal was to make a document that created a central government strong enough to keep the country together. However, it still had to address concerns of the states and have limits to its power.

WORD WISE

The Founding Fathers are the leaders who signed the Declaration of Independence, took part in the American Revolution, and wrote the Constitution.

Important Compromises

Delegates from each state had their own concerns at the convention. They debated how to balance power between the states and the national government. They also debated two plans for how the states would be represented.

Under the New Jersey Plan, each state would have the same number of representatives. This plan was better for small states. Under the Virginia Plan, the number of representatives would be based on the population of each state. This plan was better for big states. In the end, delegates agreed to the Great Compromise, which created two houses in the legislature. The Senate gave each state the same number of representatives, while the number of representatives in the House of Representatives was based on population.

Delegates met at Independence Hall. You can visit this landmark in Philadelphia, Pennsylvania.

compareandcontrast
The New Jersey Plan and Virginia Plan had different ideas about how states should be represented. Compare and contrast the two plans in terms of which states they'd benefit.

The delegates who represented Virginia at the Constitutional Convention included George Washington and James Madison.

11

There was another big debate at hand, this time between Northern and Southern states. They disagreed on whether slaves should be included in a state's population. Delegates from southern states thought that both free people and slaves should be counted in a state's population. Some delegates from northern states wanted to end slavery altogether. Some said if slavery were allowed, a state's representation should depend only on the free population.

Bringing in new slaves was already outlawed in 10 states by the time of the Constitutional Convention. However, three states still allowed it.

Southern states forced enslaved people to work on plantations, or large farms.

They decided on a compromise in which each state's representation would be based on the number of free people and three-fifths of the number of slaves in the state. This was called the Three-Fifths Compromise. Slavery would not be outlawed in the United States until 1865.

Consider This

How would it help Southern states to have their slaves counted in the population?

Three Branches

How could the writers of the Constitution create a strong central government that wouldn't become too powerful? They decided to split the government's power among three branches: the legislative, executive, and judicial branches. Each branch has a different function. Splitting the government's power is called the separation of powers.

The Constitution states that each branch of government has some power over the others. This is known as a system of checks and balances. In the system of checks and balances, the legislative branch makes laws. The executive branch can pass or reject these laws. The judicial branch can say these laws are right or wrong. The branches work together and keep one another from having absolute, or total, power.

compareandcontrast

Checks and balances ensures that the three branches of government share power so no one branch gets too powerful. Do you think that this system works well?

A Look at the Legislative Branch

The **Preamble** of the Constitution starts with "We the People of the United States." It showed that the Constitution was made by and for the people. After the Preamble, the Constitution lists articles, which each describe a part of the government or explain how the government works. Article One describes the legislative branch, known as Congress. The Constitution gives Congress the power to write laws, raise taxes, borrow money, and declare war.

The U.S. Capitol is home to both the Senate and the House of Representatives.

The Constitution has seven articles. This page shows the **Preamble** and Article One.

There are two houses of Congress. One is the Senate, which has two members from each state. The other is the House of Representatives. The number of representatives for each state is based on the state's population. The Constitution gives Congress many powers, but the executive and judicial branch can check that power.

WORD WISE

The Preamble to the Constitution is like an introduction. It explains the purpose for which the Constitution was being written.

Exploring the Executive Branch

The executive branch is described in the next article. The president is the leader of the executive branch. The president has many jobs, including being the head of the military, choosing whether to approve or veto laws passed by Congress, and appointing (choosing) people for important government jobs.

Article Two also explains checks to the executive branch's powers. The Supreme Court can decide that the president's actions are not allowed by the Constitution. The Senate must approve the people whom the president appoints. Congress can override a president's veto if enough members in each chamber vote to do so. Because of these checks, the president does not have the ability to become all-powerful like a king.

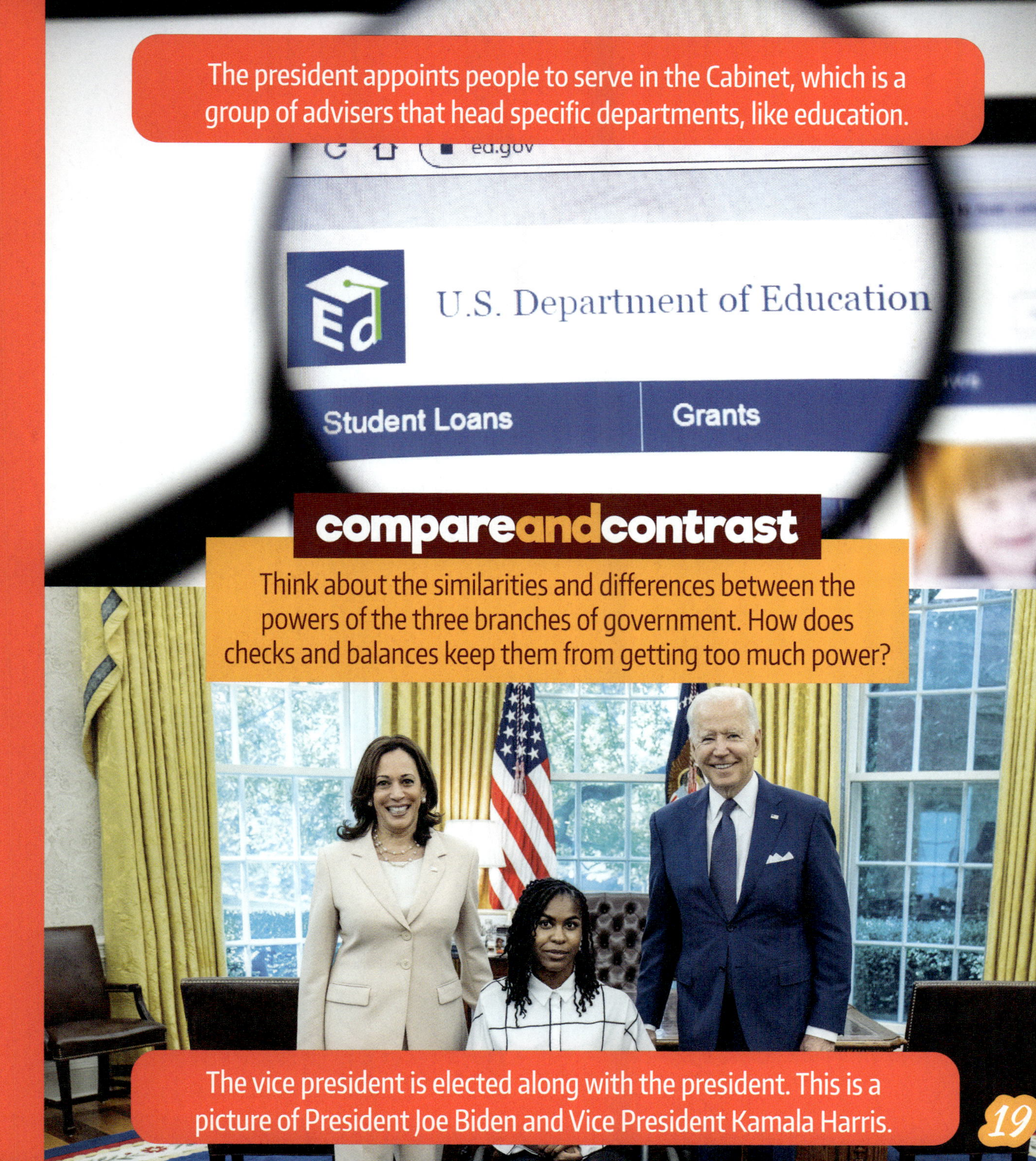

The president appoints people to serve in the Cabinet, which is a group of advisers that head specific departments, like education.

compareandcontrast

Think about the similarities and differences between the powers of the three branches of government. How does checks and balances keep them from getting too much power?

The vice president is elected along with the president. This is a picture of President Joe Biden and Vice President Kamala Harris.

Powers of the Judicial Branch

The judicial branch is organized in Article Three of the U.S. Constitution. State and federal courts make up this branch. Article Three states the kinds of cases that this court system handles.

The **Supreme Court** is the head of the judicial branch. The Supreme Court also explains the meaning of the laws in the Constitution. Justices can decide whether new or old laws agree with the Constitution or if they are unconstitutional. Unconstitutional laws are overturned.

In the Supreme Court case *Marbury v. Madison* (1803), it was decided that the courts could say if a law was unconstitutional.

The other two branches balance the judicial branch's powers. The president appoints justices to the Supreme Court, but the Senate must then approve justices. Supreme Court justices can serve for life, so this appointment and approval process is very serious.

WORD WISE

The Supreme Court can say that a state or national law is unconstitutional if that law disagrees with any part of the Constitution.

21

Limits on State Governments

Each state has its own government and makes its own laws. However, there are limits to what state governments can do. This is discussed in Article Four of the Constitution. This article says that states must respect the official acts and public records of the other states. It also says that each state's laws must treat citizens from other states the same as they do their own citizens.

Article Four also describes how new states can join the country. The most recent state to join the country was Hawaii in 1959.

Article Six made the Constitution the supreme law of the United States. It says that the Constitution and other federal laws have to be followed by every state, even if state laws on the same subject do not agree with federal laws. Article Four and Article Six helped form a stronger central government than there had been under the Articles of Confederation.

Consider This

States did not have to respect other states' laws under the Articles of Confederation. Why would this situation cause problems between states?

Amendments

The creators of the Constitution wanted to be sure that the document could be changed if needed as time went on. How to make these **amendments** is described in Article Five.

First, an amendment must be proposed. There are two ways that can happen. Two-thirds of each house of Congress can agree on an amendment, or two-thirds of the states can call for a Constitutional Convention to suggest an amendment. After an amendment has been proposed, three-fourths of the states must approve it before it is added to the Constitution.

The Thirteenth Amendment ended slavery in 1865. Juneteenth is a holiday that celebrates the day enslaved people in Texas learned they were free.

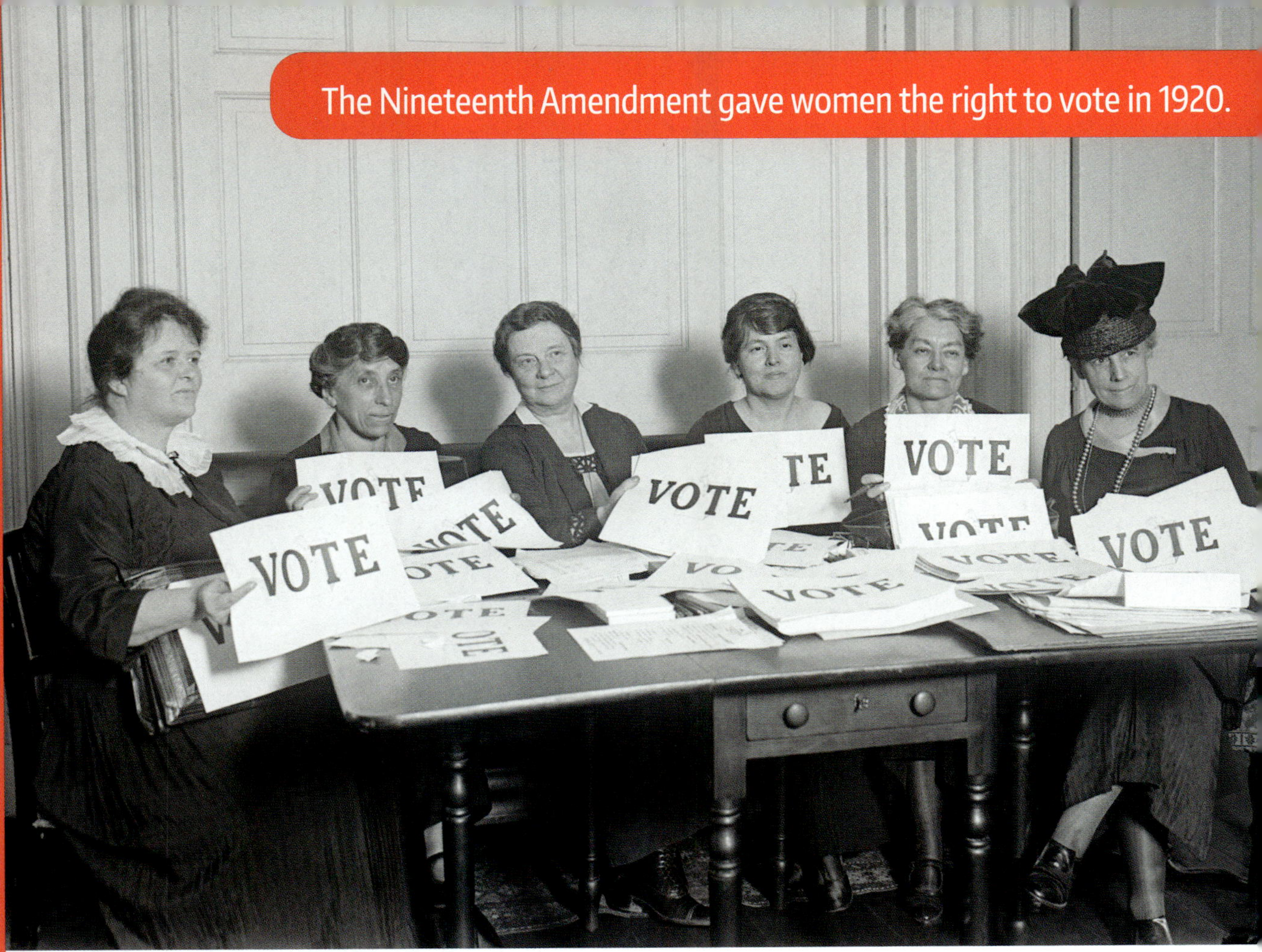

The Nineteenth Amendment gave women the right to vote in 1920.

Only 27 amendments have been added to the Constitution. Many guaranteed citizens certain rights and placed limits on the government. Some, such as the amendments that ended slavery and gave women the right to vote, moved the country forward.

WORD WISE

An amendment is a change that is made to correct a mistake.

Rights for All Citizens

Today, the rights that U.S. citizens enjoy come from a very important addition to the Constitution—the Bill of Rights. These were added to the Constitution in 1791.

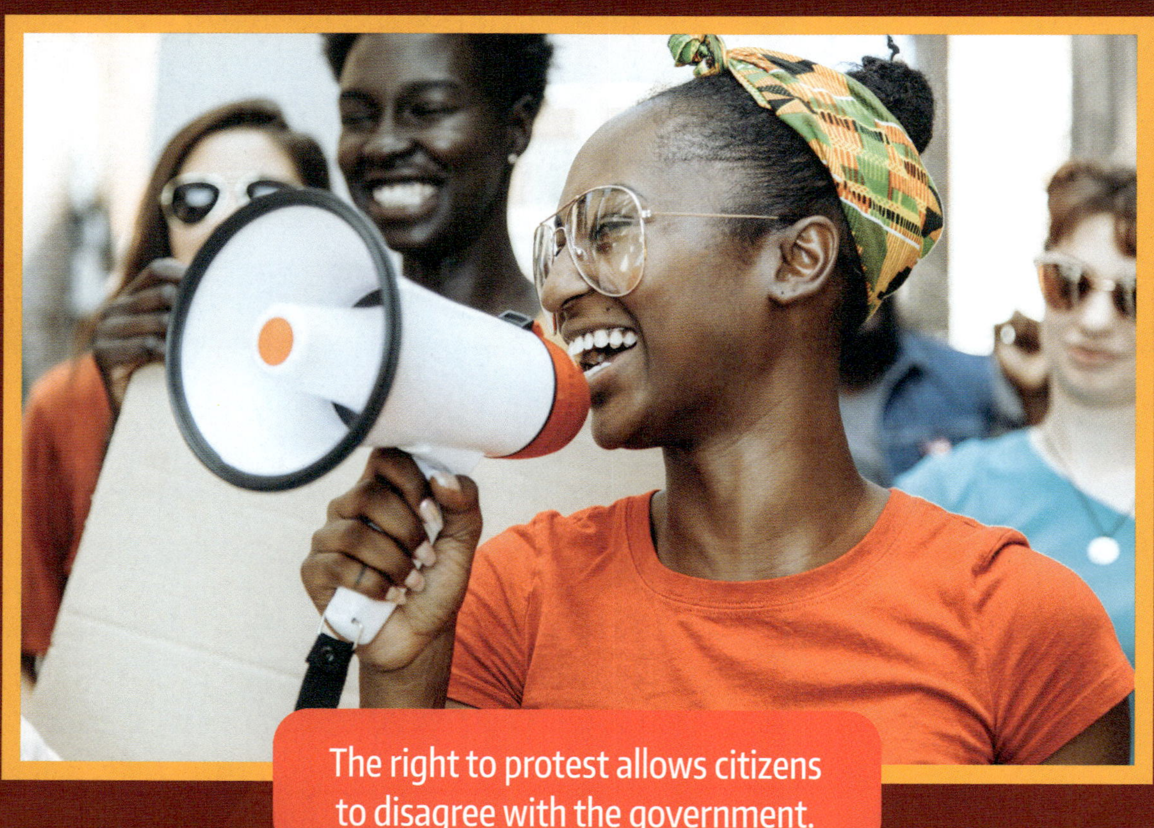

The right to protest allows citizens to disagree with the government.

The First Amendment gives the right to free speech and a free press. It also gives people the right to protest and to practice religion freely. The Second Amendment is the right to own weapons. The Fourth Amendment says that the government must have a judge's permission to search property. The Fifth, Sixth, and Seventh Amendments explain the rights a citizen has in a trial. The Eighth Amendment protects citizens from cruel punishment. The Ninth Amendment says that rights not stated in the Constitution belong to citizens. Any powers not in the Constitution were given to states or citizens, according to the Tenth Amendment.

Consider This

The Third Amendment ensured the government couldn't make citizens house soldiers. Why would this amendment make citizens feel protected after what they'd gone through as colonists?

The Road to Ratification

On September 17, 1787, delegates to the Constitutional Convention signed the U.S. Constitution. However, nine states needed to **ratify** the Constitution before it would go into effect. Ratification supporters were called Federalists, and people against ratification were Anti-Federalists. Many Anti-Federalists demanded a Bill of Rights before they'd agree to the Constitution.

Alexander Hamilton was a Federalist who helped change peoples' minds about the Constitution.

In New York, Alexander Hamilton and others wrote a series of essays known as *The Federalist Papers* to convince the New York government to ratify the Constitution. New York approved the Constitution in 1788. All thirteen states ratified the Constitution by 1790. Though the document is well over 200 years old, it's still the framework of U.S. government. The U.S. Constitution provides a peek into the past and guidelines for the present.

WORD WISE

To ratify means to approve of something legally.

Glossary

compromise: The settlement of a disagreement by each side giving up some of its demands.

Congress: The main lawmaking body of the United States. It is made up of the Senate and the House of Representatives.

Constitutional Convention: The meetings held in the summer of 1787 to create the Constitution.

debate: To discuss an issue, often publicly, by presenting and considering different ideas about that issue.

delegates: People sent with the power to vote or act for a group of people.

enforce: To carry out a law.

executive: Referring to the branch of government that carries out laws.

federal: A form of government that balances power between a national government and state governments.

House of Representatives: The part of the U.S. Congress in which the number of members a state has depends on the number of people living in that state.

judicial: Referring to the branch of the government that contains the federal court system.

justices: The nine judges on the Supreme Court are called justices. One is the chief justice. The others are associate justices.

legislative: Referring to the branch of government that writes laws. This is Congress.

protest: To display one's objection to something.

represented: To have acted for a group of people.

right: Something to which one has a just claim. In the United States, freedom of speech is a right.

Senate: The part of the U.S. Congress in which every state has the same number of members (two).

slavery: The condition in which a person is "owned" by another person.

veto: The power of the president to stop a law passed by Congress.

For More Information

Books

Levy, Janey. *The Bill of Rights: Guaranteeing Liberty*. New York, NY: Gareth Stevens Publishing, 2021.

Shea, Therese. *Team Time Machine Adds to the Bill of Rights*. New York, NY: Gareth Stevens Publishing, 2021.

Silva, Sadie. *The U.S. Constitution in Review*. Buffalo, NY: Enslow Publishing, 2023.

Websites

Bill of Rights
bensguide.gpo.gov/bill-of-rights-1789-91
Explore the Bill of Rights with this kid-friendly guide.

The Constitution
www.ducksters.com/history/us_constitution.php
Discover more facts about the U.S. Constitution and read the full Preamble.

James Madison
kids.nationalgeographic.com/history/article/james-madison
Learn more about James Madison, who is called the "Father of the Constitution."

Index